Freehand Sketching

W·W· Norton & Company · New York · London

Freehand Sketching

AN INTRODUCTION

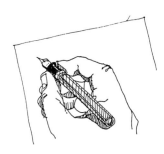

PAUL LASEAU

Drawing on page 96 by Michael Doyle, from *Color Drawing, Second Edition*, Wiley 1999.

For information about permission to reproduce selections from this book, write to Permissions, W. W. Norton & Company, Inc., 500 Fifth Avenue, New York, NY 10110

Composition by Ken Gross
Book design by Toni Krass
Manufacturing by Courier Westford
Production manager: Leeann Graham

Library of Congress Cataloging-in-Publication Data

Laseau, Paul, 1937–
    Freehand Sketching: an introduction / Paul Laseau.
        p.   cm.
    Includes index.
    ISBN 0-393-73112-X (pbk.)
    1. Architectural drawing – Technique. 2. Freehand technical sketching – Technique. I. Title.
NA2708.L37   2004
720'.28'4—dc21   2003054066

W. W. Norton & Company, Inc., 500 Fifth Avenue, New York, N.Y. 10110
www.wwnorton.com
W. W. Norton & Company Ltd., Castle House, 75/76 Wells St., London W1T 3QT

0 9 8 7 6 5 4

Credits

Unless noted otherwise, all drawings and photos are by the author. Some of the sketches by the author on pages 14–20 are based on work by students in classes and workshops conducted by the author over a period of several years. The drawings on pages 46 and 47 are based on a photo by Alfredo Fernandez-Gonzalez, Assistant Professor of Architecture, Ball State University.

The digital editing application used in chapter five is Photoshop version 7.0.

CONTENTS

INTRODUCTION

Traditionally, freehand sketching has had an important role in architectural education and practice. While digital media and developing communication technologies are bringing new tools to design, freehand sketching continues to provide unique and vital capabilities to architects and designers in allied fields.

Because appropriate design solutions must be based on extensive knowledge of the design possibilities, continuing education and research are critical parts of architectural careers. Freehand sketching provides an important tool for investigating and understanding existing and potential solutions to problems of our physical environment, such as lack of viable public social space or disorganized pedestrian and vehicular movement.

Appropriate design solutions also depend upon a productive dialogue among designers and the clients and users of environments. Such dialogues are greatly enhanced by the ability to communicate well both visually and verbally. The immediacy and informality of freehand sketching supports a relaxed and fluid conversation, and contributes to the client's confidence in a successful outcome for a project.

This book is a resource for both beginners and those returning to sketching, including traveling architects, artists, and designers setting out to discover the world around them.

The intention is to provide students with a basic guide to develop their freehand sketching skills and design instructors with a means of enriching the early design studio experience through effective instruction in freehand sketching. For individuals at any stage in their education or career, this book also offers suggestions for more effective graphic communication.

The importance of extensive reading for successful writing or extensive listening for musical composition is affirmed by writers and musicians. A parallel condition holds for visual artists—painters, sculptors, and architects. Successful artistic creativity depends upon extensive visual exposure leading to acute visual perception and imagination.

Approach

The emphasis on freehand sketching as a means to visual literacy is the thread that binds the exercises and examples throughout this book. People who sketch extensively are aware that drawing affects the way they see and that the way they see is an important factor in the effectiveness and quality of their drawings. Similarly, what you see critically affects the way you think. This relationship between sight and thought provides each of us with unique ways of drawing and thinking creatively. For these reasons, seeing and thinking should be viewed as an integral part of sketching.

To take full advantage of the versatility of sketching, you are encouraged to go beyond the subjects covered here. Just as exercises in composition and perspective are mutually reinforcing, the drawing of people and architecture or flowers and machinery brings new perceptions and increased sensitivity to each subject.

For some, the prime reason to take up sketching is to produce admirable drawings that provide a sense of accomplishment. Although such motivation is important, concern about results not only inhibits learning but also hides an even greater source of motivation: the wealth of other experiences that sketching brings. If you look carefully at the subjects you sketch, a new, exciting world of awareness and delight opens to you. For example, sketching a street may reveal how public space can be animated by:

- the acute angles of intersecting streets,
- the play of light and shadow,
- the contrast between the cool darkness under a cafe awning and the dazzling glare of the sun reflecting from the buildings in the background, and
- people—an important element in making a view stimulating.

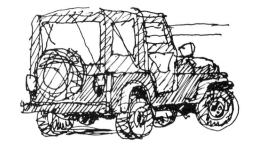

Sketching-Seeing-Sketching

Seeing what you could never see before is the unexpected bonus of sketching; it is also the key to developing drawing skills. Sketching on a regular basis provides the opportunity to practice observation. To take advantage of the opportunity, it is helpful to assume a new awareness of the visual world around you. The illustrations on this page are details of larger sketches, some of

which appear elsewhere in this book. In each instance, sketching required a close look at the subject, resulting in a new awareness—a wine glass reflecting light, the components of a jeep, the patterns of a house facade, and the peculiar configuration of a specific type of tree.

Because seeing and sketching are so interdependent, it is difficult to learn to see before beginning to sketch, and vice versa. Drawing is the key to effective seeing, and seeing is the key to effective drawing. So, where do we start? The

drawing/seeing dynamic is like a motor that needs a jump-start. Motivation is the starter for sketching—if you can derive initial interest or enjoyment from your first sketching efforts, you will begin to *see*, leading to an improvement in your sketches and increased motivation.

This book is intended to provide the necessary tools and understanding to begin sketching with a basic level of confidence. Ultimately, however, individual success in learning to sketch fluidly and competently depends heavily on practice.

This means that you must be committed to frequent freehand sketching throughout your career. Sustaining such a commitment is assured by simply deriving enjoyment from your sketching. Many an attempt to learn to draw has been thwarted by the assumption that it is a difficult but necessary task. As beneficial as drawing is to the designer, real skill develops from the pleasure that you get from drawing, not the guilt you feel about your shortcomings.

As you undertake the exercises in this book, and later as your skills progress, strive to:

- Draw only what truly interests you. You need not limit yourself to drawing the subjects in this book. Try to find subjects that inspire you.
- Accept opportunities, not obligations. If time limits, uncomfortable circumstances, or a complex subject begin to cause stress, stop and adjust your expectations as to what can be reasonably accomplished while assuring your satisfaction with the experience.
- Please yourself, not others. Finally, sketching should be seen as a continuing source of enjoyment and learning rather than a string of performances for other people. Ultimately, success in freehand sketching is a highly personal process. It must first work for you if it is ever to be useful to others.

The chapters in this book are arranged so that the reader can build skills at a reasonable pace. Beginners will want to start with the first chapter, but more advanced sketchers may start at later chapters that best meet their needs. Chapter one concentrates on immersing the reader in the act of sketching to develop basic hand-eye coordination and learn the process of "building" sketches. Chapters two and three extend sketch "building" to environmental-scale subjects found in architecture and landscape design, elaborating on the techniques of sketch construction, tone, and detail rendering. Direction for sketching a variety of environments in the field is provided in chapter four. Finally, chapter five discusses some of the possibilities for extending the application of freehand sketching through studio-based methods.

Kevin Forseth

Chapter One

BASIC SKILLS

In this chapter you will focus on building fundamental skills that support all other sketching abilities: observation and hand-eye coordination. The warm-up exercises—contour drawing and negative space depiction—will develop your ability to carefully scrutinize your drawing subjects while building your sketching confidence.

Of all the media I have used for teaching drawing, ink has been the least burdensome and the most supportive of the learning process. The permanence of ink will encourage you to always "go for it"—to try to put the line right where it should be. As you will see later, it is not usually a problem if the line lands in the wrong place, but continued attempts to accurately place lines builds the hand-eye coordination necessary for sketching. Using pencil creates a tendency to be timid, either using very faint lines or erasing bad ones. Learning to sketch is the result of continual attempts to reproduce what you see with increasing degrees of accuracy.

Simple ink line drawings will help you emphasize the content and structure of a sketch rather than its nuances. By producing a uniform line, regardless of which direction the pen is moved, the priority is to see the subject rather than decorate the drawing.

Drawing skills, like athletic skills, require constant conditioning to assure peak performance; when we fail to exercise them, we lose perception, concentration, relaxed awareness, and dexterity. In my view, technical improvements in fountain pens and fine-line markers have made them the most effective and versatile equipment for daily "workouts" in the fundamentals of artistic and design skills. These instruments are portable, durable, accessible, easy to maintain, and reliable. With practice, the

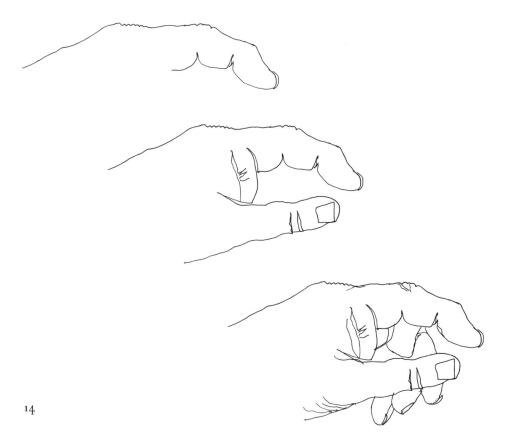

artist or designer can take advantage of the sensitivity, fluidity, precision, speed, flexibility, and economy of ink techniques.

Most of the exercises in this book can be completed with just a black fine-line marker and 5 x 8-inch blank white index cards (you may also use 8.5 x 11-inch white paper with a smooth surface, like the kind used for photocopying). General recommendations for sketching equipment can be found at the end of chapter five.

Contour Drawing

Whether you are a beginner at sketching or returning to sketching after some time has elapsed, there are certain basic exercises that help to develop or fine-tune observation skills. The first of these is contour drawing. In this exercise, use your non-drawing hand as a model (just for this exercise, it may help to tape the index card to your drawing surface). Start with the longest lines or edges. Keeping your pen on the paper and your eye on the subject, try to trace the edges and folds of your hand as if your fingers were touching them. Don't rush! With calm concentration observe and record all the changes and nuances of the forms you see. Do not be concerned if your sketches are distorted or out of proportion. The resulting sketches are not as important as building habits of concentration and observation are.

Change the position of your hand to look for interesting compositions. More time should be spent watching the subject than checking the emerging drawing. Remember that it is the process, not the result, that counts. Resist the tendency to rapidly generalize the path of lines. Gradually you will begin to notice details that you previously missed.

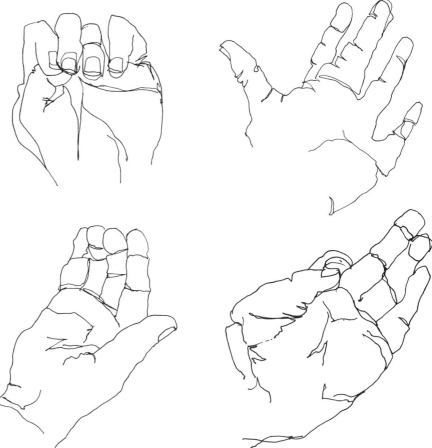

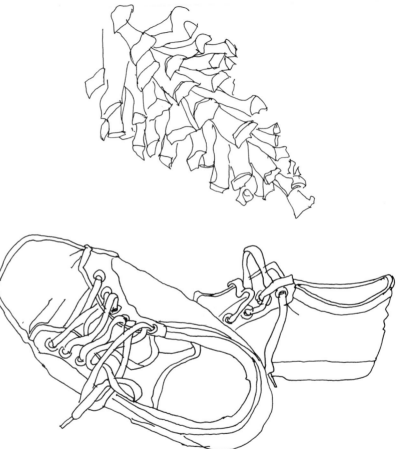

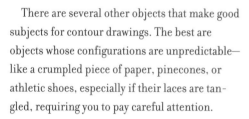

There are several other objects that make good subjects for contour drawings. The best are objects whose configurations are unpredictable—like a crumpled piece of paper, pinecones, or athletic shoes, especially if their laces are tangled, requiring you to pay careful attention.

Remember to allow yourself the luxury of looking very carefully and don't worry about the amount of time it takes to complete the drawing. These exercises train your eye to believe what you see as you try to map that in a drawing.

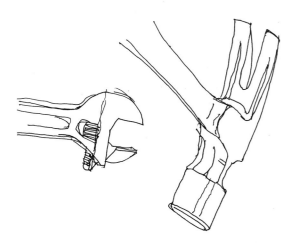

You should also experiment with man-made objects close at hand. Because of familiarity with these objects, you would think that they would be easier to sketch. Actually, assumptions you tend to make of familiar objects can distract you from looking carefully. Distractions can be reduced and sketches made more interesting by:

- choosing objects with complex curves,
- viewing the objects from unfamiliar angles, and
- placing objects in a strong light and tracing the edges of their shadows and reflections.

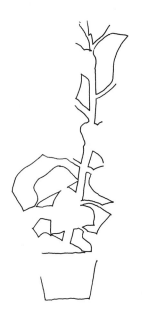

Negative Space

This form of contour drawing focuses on voids or negative spaces as an alternate way to develop concentration and hand-eye coordination. The objective of this exercise is to take your attention off of an object as a whole and concentrate on its shape and scale. You should try this approach to sketching using a variety of subjects both natural and man-made—stacked chairs, kitchen utensils, and plants are pictured here, for example. They do not have to be

large items but should have some complexity.
Magazines or newspapers are useful sources. Try
sketching from upside down images. Again, you
may find plants easier to sketch than man-made
objects because there is less temptation to
assume you know what the shapes are, and you
will be forced to look more carefully.

Try to trace the edges of the forms as you see
them. Drawing from nature requires a good deal
of patience, so be sure to give yourself time to
look, observe, and draw.

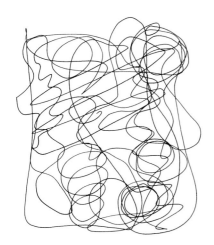

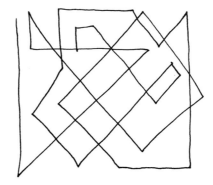

Getting Comfortable with Sketch Media

The exercises in this book, and sketching in general, are best done in a relaxed state. When you feel tense or hesitant, try overcoming these barriers by engaging a whole sheet of paper with your pen. Touch your pen to the surface and allow it to move about randomly in all directions and in different types of strokes. Alternatively, without changing the orientation of the sheet, move the pen in straight lines in all directions.

Hand-eye coordination can be improved by the spiral exercise: start at the outside and in a continuous motion draw several rings ending at the center. The objective is to draw as many rings as you can, as fast as you can, without having the lines touch each other. Try drawing different size spirals in both clockwise and counterclockwise directions.

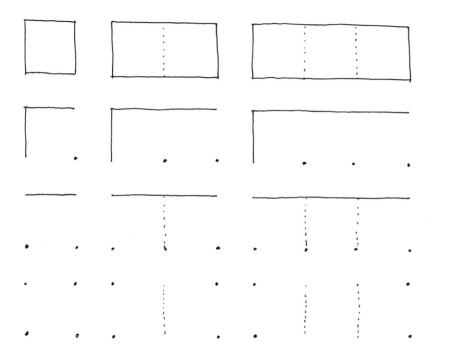

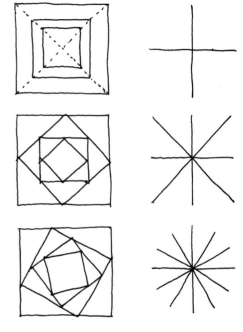

This exercise helps with your coordination and your sense of proportion and scale, skills that play an important role in sketching.

The rectangles above are of different proportions based on the module of a square. The goal is to establish their proportions with a diminishing presence of graphic marks (the dotted lines are added later to check the accuracy of the attempts).

The diagrams to the right again test your sense of the square and exercise your ability to make subdivisions of lines or space—in halves in the second row and in thirds in the third row. The last diagram (far right) corresponds to the familiar hour positions on a clock, an awareness that will come in handy in later exercises. Comparing

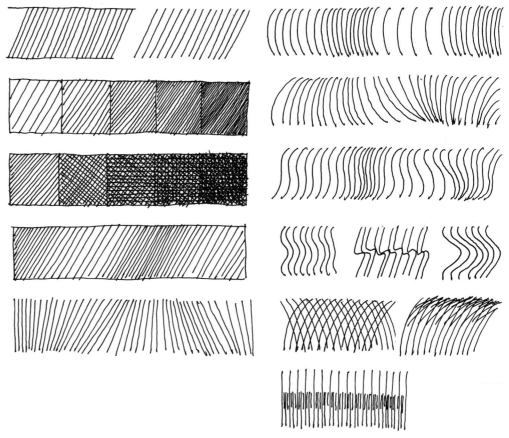

your sketch to the angles of hands on a clock can help to create a line representing an edge you observe.

The exercises on this page address consistency of strokes. Try to keep the lines going in the same direction while evenly spacing them. At first, use guidelines above and below to control the length of your lines; then, try these strokes without guidelines. Varying the distance between lines has the effect of creating tones of different darkness, which will be useful for rendering sketches later on.

Building Sketches

Now that you are beginning to feel comfortable sketching, you are ready for exercises in a basic process that will help you complete sketches of any size or subject.

The sketching process upon which this book is based is designed to directly address common impediments to learning how to sketch—feeling overwhelmed by the complexity of the subject and the perceived amount of work required, and not knowing where to start. The process provides a plan of attack for building a sketch. Your sketching task is made feasible by organizing it into several smaller, less threatening tasks arranged in a sequence to minimize the occurrence of common mistakes and to maximize effectiveness.

The three basic sketching tasks are as follows:
- constructing the sketch
- modeling space and form with tone
- indicating details and pattern

As we address each of these three basic skills, it is important to keep in mind that all sketching requires a concentrated look at the subject. The objective is to draw what you actually *see*, not what you think you *know*.

Construction

Tone

Detail

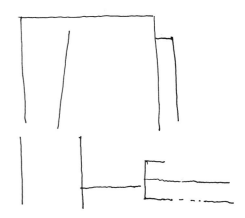

For your initial sketch you can use this photo and/or objects close at hand that engage you (consider making interesting arrangements of them). In addition to setting up your sketch subject, you are beginning the important process of scanning your surroundings to discover what moves you.

Construct your view slowly and sketch major edges first. Constantly check the match between your sketch and the subject. The placement of these first lines affects the success of the rest of the sketch. When you have finished this step

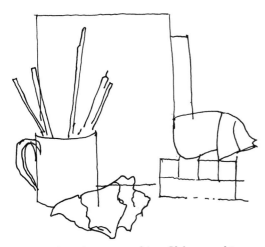

compare it again to your subject. If there are big differences, start a new sketch.

Next, add other lines or contours based on their relationship to the previous lines. To properly position the angles of the pencils or the edges of the shadows you can either note where the lines begin and end or compare them to positions of the hands on a clock. If you have done a good job with the first step, these additions should be comparatively easy, but remember to look carefully at your subject.

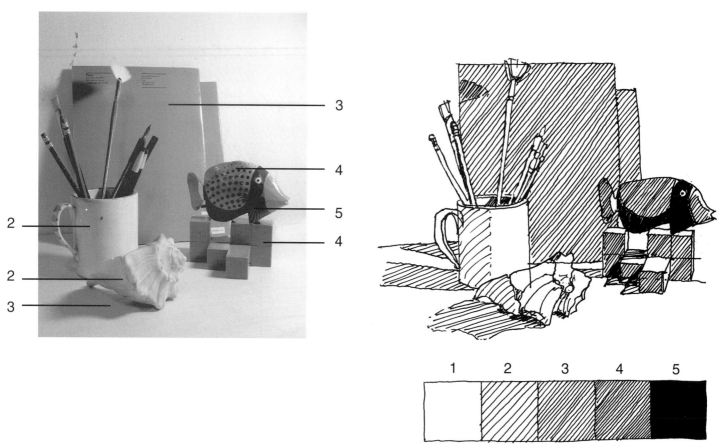

Applying Tone and Detail

At this stage tones are applied to the sketch using a repetition of parallel lines. Start by studying your subject to discern at least five levels of darkness, including white and black. Draw five boxes in which to indicate the range of tones to be used in the sketch. The middle three gray tones are created by varying the distance between lines. When you are satisfied you have drawn three distinct levels of gray that emulate those in the subject, apply the tones in a similar manner to the sketch. Generally speaking, the lines are drawn on a diagonal to avoid confusion with the edges of forms or their shadows.

Porta Settimiana
10/22 2:45 pm.

Villa Farnesina down
this street.

Carcofi in
courtyard.

Porta Settimiana, Rome
Frank Ching

Chapter Two

ENVIRONMENT: SKETCH CONSTRUCTION

Embedded in environments is the history of our planet and the drama of human evolution. Whether you are a professional designer or simply expanding your awareness of environments, there are endless opportunities for discovery. Whether you are traveling to other lands and cultures or exploring your own hometown, sketching provides an effective and convenient means to absorb the richness of lessons that environment may provide.

Now that the process of building a sketch is familiar, you are ready to tackle the more complex subject of environments. For convenience, the subject of sketching environments has been divided into two chapters—Sketch Construction and Sketch Tone and Detail. In both chapters you will undertake exercises that you can do at home or in a studio. You will sketch from pictures or slides, an accessible and convenient way to start your sketching practice. This is advantageous because it offers you access to a range of interesting subjects and views which have already been selected, cropped, and flattened into two-dimensional form. Not only are slides and photographs less intimidating than drawing directly from observing three-dimensional objects, they also provide access to a greater variety of subjects than may be readily available nearby.

It is best to start sketch construction studies at a small scale, about the size of a playing card. Begin by carefully drawing a rectangle representing the edge of the photograph or slide. Practice drawing rectangles at the appropriate proportions to avoid distortion in your sketch composition. Always work from larger to smaller shapes as if you were making a map of the sketch's general outline and then its sub-elements.

Distorted frame

Distorted frame

At each step refer back to the photo to check your level of accuracy. If you feel you have misplaced a line, redraw the line in its appropriate position. If you find these first lines are getting out of control or becoming too complex, it is best to restart the sketch. Remember

these are drawings designed to build skill rather than create fine-tuned images.

Note: Perspective construction techniques are purposely avoided in this chapter. While perspective is a handy device to construct imagined spaces, it is

Properly proportioned frame

not useful, and possibly detrimental, to sketching existing environments. Using perspective can place an arbitrary screen between you and the environment, leading to rationalizing rather than scrutinizing your subject.

Sub-elements added

Final construction

33

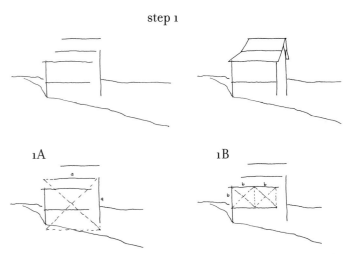

step 1

1A

1B

Sketch Building Example

Working with a slide of a barn and hillside, first draw a rectangle the same proportion as the 35 mm slide (2:3). Begin constructing the sketch by identifying significant vertical and horizontal edges (step 1). This important step requires positioning the major shapes as accurately as possible. Note that the horizon line starts at the right edge of the frame about two-fifths from the bottom, and the right edge of the barn is just shy of the middle of the width of the frame. Images 1A and 1B demonstrate an alternate way to verify proportions by overlaying squares. Once the major shapes are complete, add smaller shapes, or sub-elements, such as windows and doors within them (step 2).

In the third step tones are added using hatching—diagonal lines of different densities. Usually tones are created with diagonal hatching throughout to avoid confusion with the orthogonal lines of the drawing. These tones provide a sense of the volume of the barn as it appears in daylight.

step 2   step 3   step 4

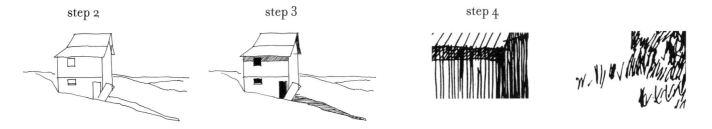

Detail and texture are applied in the fourth step of the drawing. In this case, details include the barn siding, the ridges on the metal roof, and the grass at the base of the barn. You will notice that the density of the lines indicating wood siding on the right side of the barn creates a darker tone. As you draw certain objects you should be aware of the tonal value of certain details and adjust your line densities accordingly.

Grids, Frames, and Shapes

This section includes exercises in using all three of the convenient devices for initial construction of sketches—grids, frames, and shapes. Each device is a way of subdividing the sketch into areas to facilitate the estimates of distances and angles. While the examples are set up so that you can sketch directly from them, you are encouraged to also work from slides of subjects that particularly interest you.

GRID EXERCISE ONE

Using the drawing on page 36 as your subject, construct a basic drawing using the three steps on this page. Though seemingly simple, each step needs careful attention. Start with the rectangle that frames the view (2:3).

1. Locate and draw a few significant horizontal and vertical edges, paying close attention to their position within the picture frame (you might decide to compare their distance from the edge of the picture frame to its total width, i.e. 1/3, 1/4). Be sure to compare your result with the sketching subject before proceeding to the next step.

2. Add sub-elements to the sketch, including the tank, fences, and the barn door, using the initial framework of lines to help position them and check their proportions.

3. Add additional details such as the patterns of barn roofing, siding, and fence rails. Indicate the edges of shadows and you are done.

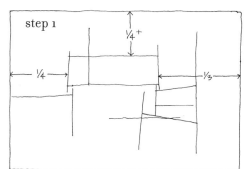

step 1

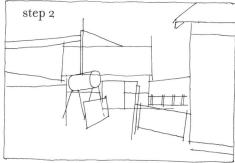

step 2

step 3

Unity Temple, Oak Park, Illinois
Frank Lloyd Wright, architect

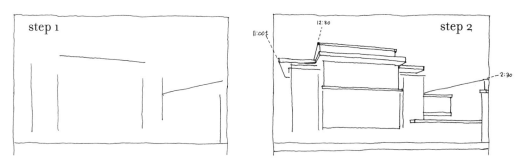

GRID EXERCISE TWO

The sketch building process in this example follows the same three steps as the previous example. This subject may be slightly more difficult because of your tendency to rationalize what you see in terms of geometry and perspective. Try to forget notions of perspective and trust your eye. If you draw lines where you see them they will automatically be "in perspective." In the second drawing the angle of slanted lines is achieved by imagining the lines as hands on a clock.

Frame Exercise One

Some subjects—paths, streets, or interior spaces—lend themselves to the use of frames to build a sketch. The process is still basically one of constructing large divisions of the view and then subdividing.

1. Sketch the largest frame, closest to you, formed by the outline of the trees. Add the square of the building facade and the pointed archway that leads to the courtyard. These frames divide the view into a foreground, middle ground, and background.

2. Outline the sub-elements—windows, doors, etc.

3. Complete the sketch construction by outlining areas where shadows will be added later.

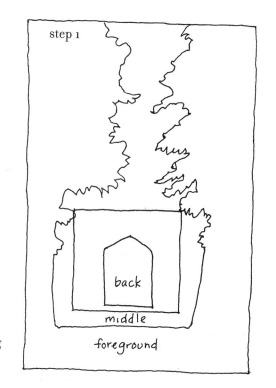

step 1

back

middle

foreground

step 2

step 3

41

FRAME EXERCISE TWO

For this sketch you will apply frames to a slightly more complex subject—an urban street. Carefully survey your subject to identify significant frames. In this example the largest frame is formed by a tree and the corner of a building in the foreground. Begin by sketching these frames and considering their position in relation to the overall view. Next, using the frames as a guide, add sub-elements as in the last exercise. If you find that the sketch becomes too dense to clearly include details, try making a larger sketch on a letter-size sheet of paper.

step 1

step 2

step 3

43

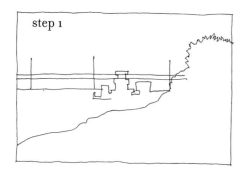

step 1

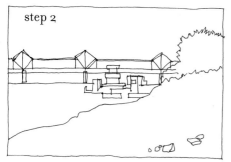

step 2

step 3

SHAPE EXERCISE ONE

The illustrations above depict a dominant or unusual form to demonstrate the third composi-tional device, shape. In this example, the river-bank and bridge establish the organization of all the other elements of the view.

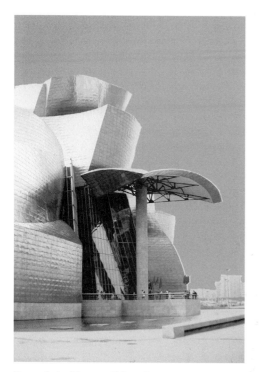

Guggenheim Museum, Bilbao, Spain
Frank Gehry, architect

SHAPE EXERCISE TWO

For this subject you will use a combination of grid and shape techniques to construct your sketch. Careful placement of the large column within the picture frame is key to the positioning of just about everything else. With the column in place, you might continue by setting the two curves immediately above and then add a few other significant curves. If this is successful, the rest of the sketch will be relatively easy.

step 1

step 2

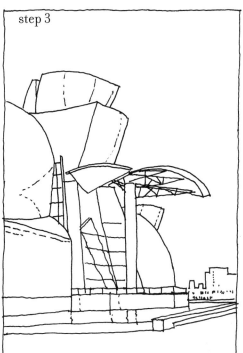

step 3

47

Amboise
Le Clos-Luce
De Vinci Home
5/10/00

Leonardo DaVinci's house, Amboise
Tim White

Chapter Three

ENVIRONMENT: SKETCH TONE AND DETAIL

When you have grounding in the basic skills of composition and construction and their importance to successful sketches, it is time to gain an understanding and experience of the roles of tone and detail in bringing sketches to their full expression. In general terms, tone conveys the three-dimensionality of environments by representing the interaction of form and light. Details can reveal qualities of materials and methods of fabrication or construction.

In this chapter, tone and detail are treated together because their representations frequently overlap. The density of lines needed to show a tile roof pattern or vertical siding may create sufficient darkness of tone so that no additional tonal hatching is necessary. On the other hand, the contrast between shadow and light may be sufficiently severe that details of materials in shadow need not be rendered.

The techniques presented in this chapter are based on the choice of ink as the sketch medium for reasons discussed earlier. While ink lines can be particularly efficient in capturing details, there are some drawbacks or limitations. For example, the use of hatching to create tone can sometimes be tedious and time consuming. You should keep in mind that this approach to building sketching skills focuses on the importance of observation and hand-eye coordination. Effective hatching requires a conscious determination of the range of tonal values present in your sketch subject in order to select the appropriate spacing of hatching lines to create representative tones. The continuous use of controlled hatching will build your dexterity.

Tone

Space and form are revealed to us through the patterns of tone created by light. Sketching is often our first opportunity to become fully aware of the range of values (light to dark) of tones and their impact on our perception of the visual world.

Consider the impact of tone and detail applied to this sketch of a village. See how a sense of space and scale emerges from the simple outline of buildings. If you get in the habit of sketching, you will discover similar examples in a wide variety of settings. The character of the facade of a building (opposite), for example, often depends upon the play of shadows and the high tonal contrast between the windows and walls. The wide range of subtle patterns in the leaves of a tree is almost entirely visible through variations in tone.

In applying tone to specific sketches, it is important to first distinguish different sources of

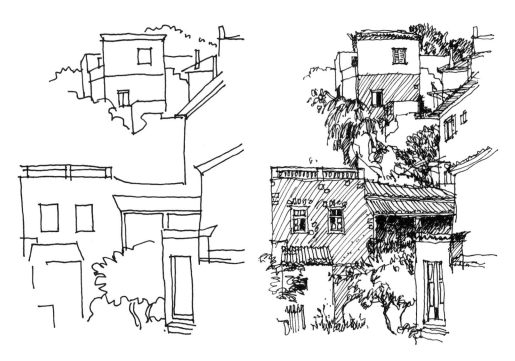

50

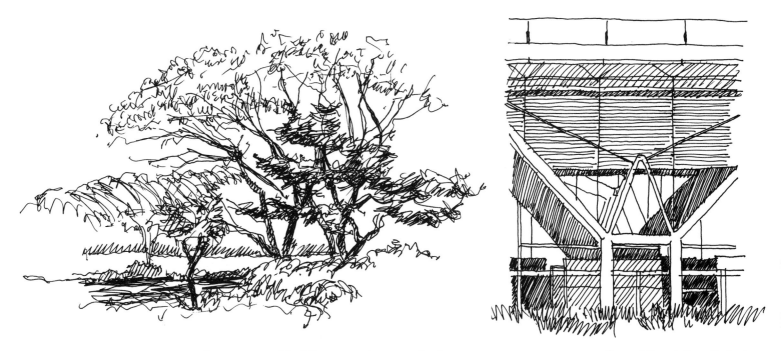

Stansted Airport, Essex, England
Foster and Partners, architects

tone: the tones created by the density of a texture, such as bark on a tree, roofing on a house, or stones in a garden wall; the tones created by color; and the tones of shade and shadow created by the reflection of light upon forms.

The following sections cover the three sources of tonal variation in environments—texture, color, shade and shadow. Multiple examples are provided to illustrate methods of applying different sources of tone, alone or in combination.

Texture

There are a variety of techniques for indicating texture, ranging from the literal depiction of patterns of foreground subjects to the more abstract depiction of texture for distant surfaces. You will find many choices of technique in this section and elsewhere in the book, and you should also note the techniques used by other architectural illustrators.

The dividing line between texture and color can often be muddied when the sketcher is producing tone. Brick, for example, is often rendered as tightly packed horizontal lines. The

lines may recall the horizontal rows of brick but
they also produce a gray tone, and this may cause
the brick to appear too dark in color. When representing dense textures such as brick, it is
important to be aware of the tonal values they
create. If the resulting value is too dark for the
color of the surface, you may have to eliminate or
greatly reduce indications of texture; a slight
variation in rendering texture may suffice. If the
density of the texture indication does not produce a dark enough tone, the area can be dark-
ened with additional hatching.

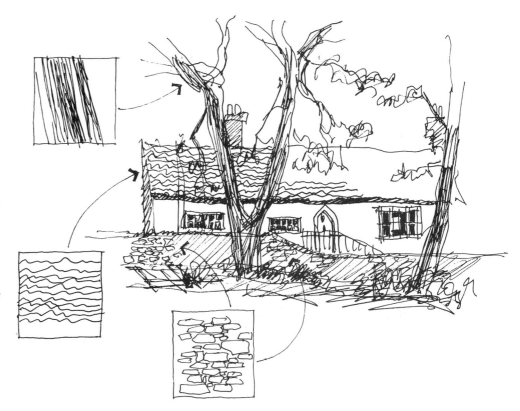

Color

Representing color in the black-and-white medium of a sketch may seem a considerable challenge. However, color theory generally recognizes three attributes, the last of which is achieveable in a black-and-white medium: hue, intensity, and value. *Hue* is the distinguishing attribute of color represented by the color wheel—namely red, blue, orange, and so on.

Troy House, Taos, NM, Antoine Predock, architect

Intensity is the amount of color present—pink is a red of low intensity, for example; gray is a combination of colors of very low intensity. The third attribute of color, *value*—the lightness or darkness of a color—can be effectively rendered in black-and-white media.

While value is a very important attribute of color as it appears in objects or environments, it is the least appreciated. As the tavern sign on the facing page illustrates, sharp contrasts in value are an important means by which color achieves emphasis and interest. On the other hand, a wide range of values like those in the sketch of the house above can convey much of the subtlety of color found in landscapes.

When you first begin to sketch, it is often difficult to discern the relative values of color because of all the other information and associations that colors convey. Squinting is the quickest way to begin to sort out values. In order to distinguish color from texture, color tones should usually be applied diagonally on surfaces to avoid confusion with the edges of the surfaces or indications of texture. Texture marks are generally smaller in scale with breaks, whereas color hatching covers a wider area of the sketch in a continuous manner. There is no precise formula, however. Easch sketch must be handled to distinguish the two forms. Practice producing value ranges, such as those shown on the facing page, may improve your skill. As you gain sketching experience, you will want to try different approaches to indicating color-generated tones.

55

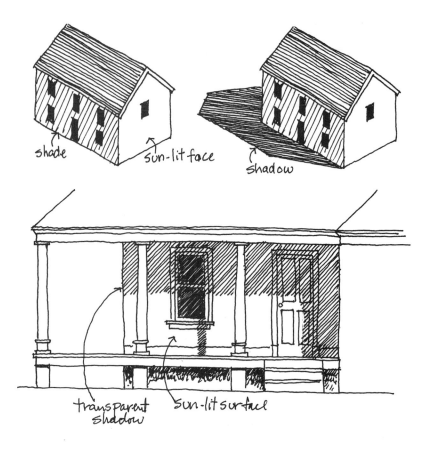

shade

sun-lit face

shadow

transparent shadow

sun-lit surface

Shade and Shadow

The last sources of tone to be applied are those created by the reflection of light on forms or spaces. Shade is generally a relatively dark area to be found on the surface of objects that do not receive direct light. Shadow is a dark area cast onto sunlit surfaces by objects that block light. Except in cases of extreme contrast, both shade and shadow are transparent; that is, we can usually see details and textures within the areas of darkness with varying degrees of clarity. In order to convey this transparency, you should draw shade and shadow tones at an angle to both texture and color indications wherever possible.

Viewed up close, shade and shadow are often not uniform in tone or density. One way to render subtle shifts in tone is to add layers of hatching at different angles. Another approach is to use shorter strokes of varying density over the more uniform hatching of color or texture.

Try duplicating the shadow effects in the barn sketch to the right. Sketch the interesting shadow and/or shade effects you find in photos.

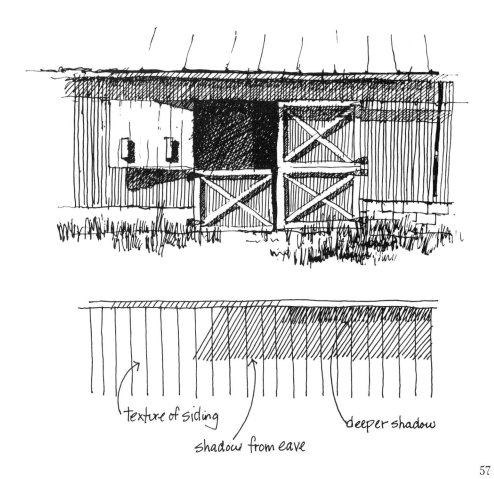

texture of siding

shadow from eave

deeper shadow

Shape and Volume

Because of the ways in which objects of different shapes and materials intercept, reflect, or distort light, tone is instrumental in depicting shape and volume. Variations in tone can be subtle and often defy analysis. It is important to render them just as they are seen, paying particular attention to detail configurations of tone, such as the edges of shadows cast on the ground by the water casks to the right. Although longer parallel-line tones may be used, short stroke techniques are often more effective.

Before applying tone to represent shape or volume in larger, environmental subjects, carefully study the subtle variations in tone. Note in the example opposite that the shaded surfaces are typically lighter than the cast shadows.

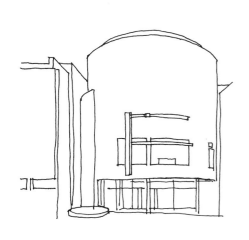

Museum of Contemporary Art, Barcelona, Spain, Richard Meier, architect

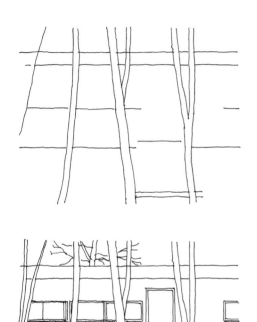

The exercise on this page will teach you to sketch several sources of tone—texture, color, shade, and shadow. Using this house as your model, build the sketch according to the three steps outlined in chapter two. Then, indicate shade and shadow, followed by texture. Note that the house is rather modest and straightforward in its design, but the rhythm of the trees and the play of shadows add interest and energy to the view. This sketch demonstrates how the experience of architecture is often influenced by context.

Caesar Cottage, Lakeville, CT, Marcel Breuer, architect

The sketches on the next two pages illustrate different ways to apply tone. You can use them as models to practice tone rendering techniques. More important, you should do some investigating on your own by noting the different impacts of light and shadow, and recording textures and patterns.

Saynatsalo Town Hall, Saynatsalo, Finland
Alvar Aalto, architect

The next three sketches demonstrate an attempt to achieve a balance between the rendering of tone and detail. Frequently this balance is influenced by the interests or perceptions of the sketchers as they react to their subjects. In the sketch of the temple entrance on this page, the details of the shapes and textures take precedence over the rendering of light and shadow. On the opposite page, the vignette of the garden gate depends heavily on the rendering of shadow, whereas the waterfront sketch focuses on the vivid contrast between light and dark and the resulting reflections.

Detail and Pattern

Much of the quality or character of a subject can be conveyed through carefully sketched details, where your powers of observation are most severely taxed. To promote success and enjoyment in sketching, approach each drawing as if it is a mystery and you are the detective looking for clues. When you first pick out a subject to sketch, you may sense that it is intriguing or stimulating. Sketching is your investigation of the source of those qualities. If you succeed, the qualities will be reflected in the sketch, and you will become a better detective.

Details tell us much about a subject: the inherent qualities of the materials—soft, brittle, slippery, coarse, smooth, heavy, or light; the way the subject was constructed, joined, or fashioned; the effects of climate and nature over time; and the ways in which the subject is or has been used.

Approach to Detail

Often the amount of detail in the view you are sketching can be overwhelming. If you dwell on the apparent vastness of your task, you can become worn out before you start. To avoid this problem, remember your role as a detective— seek out the specific details that are the basis for a pattern. These details might be the typical method of laying brick or stone, the arrangement of leaves in a tree or plant, overlapping straw in a basket, divisions in a window, or wrinkles on a face. Carefully record the detail, including written notes where helpful, then pursue the rest of the detail at a time when you feel less pressed. Often when you return to a sketch to insert textures and patterns, your enthusiasm will be renewed and your perceptions enriched. Although much of the charm of a sketch may be found in the spontane- ity of immediate reactions to a subject, some- times postponing completion brings a detach- ment that can introduce important refinements.

The sketches on this page illustrate how framing areas of rich detail increases their impact on our experience of environment.

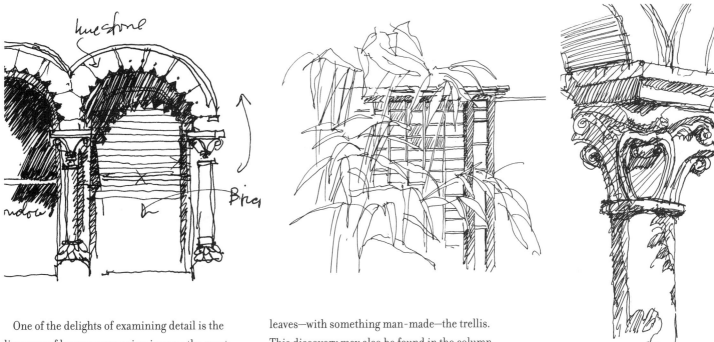

One of the delights of examining detail is the discovery of human expression in even the most commonplace items, such as window openings or columns. As the three illustrations above demonstrate, this might include the limestone "teeth" of an archway or the juxtaposition of nature—the leaves—with something man-made—the trellis. This discovery may also be found in the column to the right. The specific form of the capital is unnecessary to support the arches above, but the detail reflects the pleasure the designer took in going beyond simple function.

69

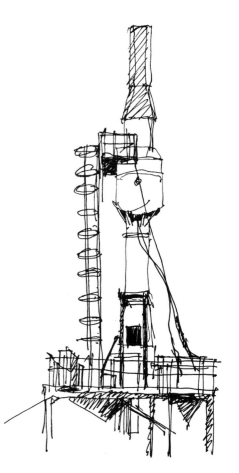

Sketching details requires concentration and can be time consuming, at times, even tedious. Therefore, it is worth the effort to find interesting detail subjects before starting to draw. Once you get in the habit of looking, you will find many possibilities. Good subjects may not be far away, but hiding in places to which you don't usually pay attention. For example, the subjects on these pages were found in a cemetery, an abandoned factory, a chimney, a front porch, and a garden.

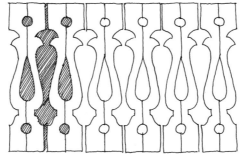

Practice with each of these subjects, or ones like them, expands your knowledge of form and contributes to your accessible graphic vocabulary. Educators have also noticed that the sus-tained concentration required of detail sketching often carries over into the design process in the studio, where intense focus is required.

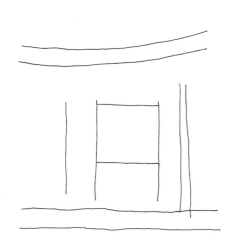

The exercise illustrated on these two pages challenges you to put all the sketch elements—construction, tone, and detail—together. Construct the sketch from scratch using the grid technique, and follow the steps outlined on page 32. After you have added the major tones to the sketch, you are ready to add the details. With all the other elements in place, sketching details should be less intimidating. Take your time and carefully observe the final version of the sketch.

Upon completing this final exercise on environmental sketching, you should be ready to find subjects that are particularly interesting and challenging for you in the field. Certainly travel provides a wealth of opportunity to enjoy sketching and its personal rewards. If your experience is anything like that of many students and practitioners who have earnestly taken up sketching, your sensitivity to and enjoyment of environments will be greatly enhanced. The next chapter will help you make the most of these opportunities.

South Beach Revetment, Bermuda, 1992, Paul Stevenson Oles, renderer

Chapter Four

SKETCHING IN THE FIELD

The previous chapters were devoted to developing your sketching skills, interest, and confidence to support the ultimate goal of being able to sketch what you want, where you want, and when you want. This chapter provides a practical guide to sketching in a variety of circumstances in the field.

The most practical and effective way to get in the habit of sketching in the field is to purchase a sketchbook. Specific recommendations about portable sketchbooks can be found at the end of this chapter. Find a sketchbook that best suits you and carry it with you—sketch subjects or design ideas may pop up unexpectedly, so you want to be prepared. Some designers leave their sketchbooks nearby when they sleep in order to record images that come to them in dreams or just as they awake.

Try to develop a habit of sketching frequently. Just fifteen or twenty minutes twice a week will produce great results. Find a quiet, comfortable place where you will not be interrupted. Select or set up an interesting subject. Turn off your cell phone if you have one. Put on earphones and music. If you are distracted by concerns about time, hide clocks and watches and try using an egg timer.

Keep your sketches in a folder so you can look at your progress from time to time. Remember that these sketches are for your private enjoyment and development.

You will find sketching in the field an interesting and exhilarating experience. Often people will look over your shoulder in admiration or with a range of comments. With practice, you can be as unobtrusive or interactive with bystanders as you wish.

View Selection

Looking for an interesting view of an environment is as important as making the drawing itself. A stimulating subject can be a catalyst for environmental education and motivation to complete the drawing. Take time to walk around your potential subject and examine the variety of visual experiences it provides. Trust your eye. Chances are quite good that what you find interesting has embedded features from which you can learn. Drawing is as much about seeing and reacting as about manual skill.

View Framing

Selecting a frame for the view you intend to sketch aids considerably in the construction of a sketch. Generally, this would be a rectangular frame, either horizontal or vertical. For any given view there are often several framing possibilities from which to make a selection. In selecting the frame for the view, you will also become aware of certain qualities of the subject and the view: balance, emphasis, contrast, verticality, horizontality, and tension. This awareness will not only help in selecting the view but also in rendering tone and detail to complete your sketch.

Selecting a view of a subject and composing elements within that view takes practice. Carry an empty photographic slide mount with you. When you have selected a direction from which to view your subject, use the slide mount to establish a frame for the view you wish to sketch. Experiment with both horizontal and vertical orientations.

With a clear idea of your subject and the way in which you wish to frame your view, you can proceed with the remaining steps—sketch construction and the rendering of tone and detail, as shown on the following pages. The frame you chose for your view can be used as an orienting device to construct your sketch. For this barn subject, for example, the tree standing at the left of the frame has a major branch that begins to protrude just above half of the height of the frame. Horizontal and vertical edges of the barn can be positioned in a similar way. Tone and detail rendering are shown by the illustrations on the opposite page.

Observation

For the average person, simple enjoyment of environment is an ample reward. Designers, however, must go beyond enjoyment to under-stand environments. They must develop a keen awareness of the variety of components of successful designs. As a researcher, the designer needs to be both an investigator and a discoverer. Typically, this means examining environment from a particular point of view, but also being open to noticing the unexpected.

Equally interesting as the windmill to the left is the anticipation of the view as you ascend the grass-covered steps. On the facing page, the sketch of the window, even in its rough state, conveys the stabilizing effect of its symmetrical and hierarchical design. The sketch of the sky-line demonstrates that environment has an impact at some distance as well as up close. The umbrellas left by customers in the entrance to a store remind us of the importance of traces of human activity to environmental experience. All of these observed effects are potential "tools" in a designer's repertoire.

A healthy approach to the research and development of observation skills involves taking on a broad range of subjects and points of view. Inspiration and challenge can be found in some of the strangest places, such as the view through a window (above). The frames of the window mullions stand in strong contrast to the vibrant curves of the tree beyond. This sketch also reveals the power of a limited view to stir our imagination. The sketch of the fishing shack and coast beyond illustrates the powerful contrast between near and far views.

Editing

While it is important to see the details of a subject, it is not necessary to render all of them. A sketch never can and never should be identical to its subject. As a two-dimensional object intended to be viewed at close range, a sketch has its own requirements as a communicating artifact. Although the subject is the basis of the message conveyed by a sketch, the effectiveness of the communication depends to an extent on manipulating the media of the sketch. If, for example, the entire pattern is fully rendered, the result may be a boring, monotonous, or lifeless sketch. If the process of sketching the pattern is equally boring, it could affect your attitude and thereby other parts of the sketch. In communication terms, too much noise has entered the system; the dominance of the pattern has obscured other messages in the sketch. But, if you apply pattern or detail so as to support your interest and insight in the subject, the result is often more interesting to the viewer.

At times, you may even leave areas of a sketch blank. These open areas can be useful to the composition, leading the viewer's eye around the sketch or creating a stimulating tension. Omission of information can also be a means of involving viewers, engaging their imagination to consider the possibilities or to supply the missing information.

Responding to Context

A sketch is realized partly by circumstance and partly by your interests. It was immediately evident to me that the hovercrafts in this illustration would make a fantastic subject for a sketch, but justice could not be done to the subject in the limited time available. The solution: Take a few pictures with a small, pocket-sized camera for future reference. Capture some of the main points of interest with a quick sketch, then construct the final sketch back in the studio.

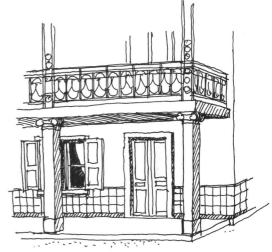

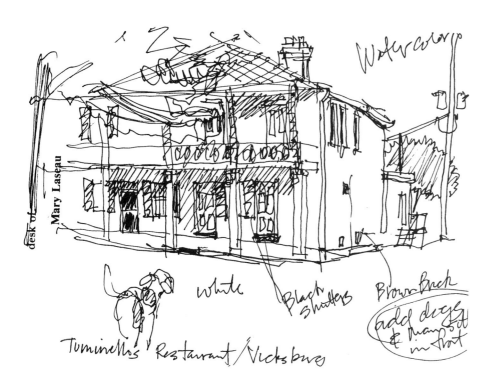

desk of

Mary Laseau

Watercolors

white

Black Shutters

Brown Brick

add dogs & man out in front

Tuminello's Restaurant / Vicksburg

To the left is a quick on-site sketch of a restaurant made under severe time constraints. Rather than attempt the impossible task of accurately sketching everything, the general disposition of the building was noted and accompanied by written notes about some of its features. Then, a typical segment of the building was singled out for more detailed notation (above). These sketches were sufficient to permit construction of a more complete drawing of the restaurant at a later time.

85

Trees

Trees are probably the most common natural element of entourage you will include in sketches. Here are some rules of thumb: Render trees differently depending on their distance from you (see sketch opposite). In close-up views, carefully draw edges and detail. In mid-distance views, draw their general shape with a hint of texture. And, for trees in the far distance, just show simple, overall shapes with the addition of tone as appropriate.

The best aid for learning to sketch trees is to work from actual environments. From time to time, however, examples such as those opposite may be useful.

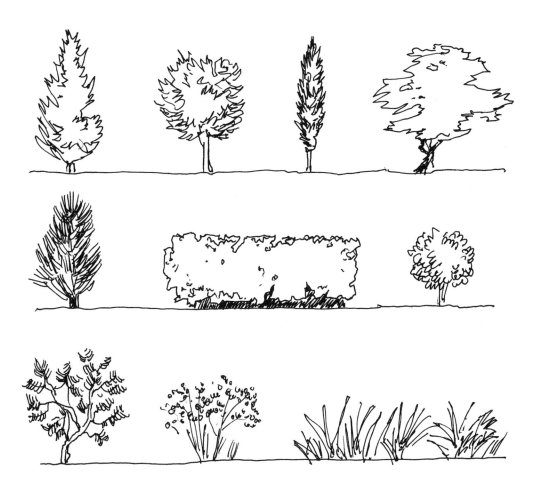

People

In general, people are one of the most difficult subjects to sketch. First of all, people are usually moving. Second, we are often intimidated by the detail of faces and hands. Start by sketching people who are seated with their backs to you. Concentrate on the large shapes or edges, then add the smaller shapes, tone, and details. For faces, you might sketch profiles before attempting frontal views. Tracing figures from photos in magazines can help develop your knowledge of human forms and build your confidence. Try to work quickly and don't be too judgmental about your efforts. Enjoy the variety of people you encounter.

Try to include people in your environment sketches whenever you can to add a sense of scale and activity. The sketch above shows that sometimes capturing a moment in which people react to their environment is more important than recording the details of their appearance.

Keeping a Journal

Many creative people, whether designers, artists, writers, or inventors, have found keeping a journal a significant aid to personal development. Regular daily or weekly entries that record thoughts, inspirations, problems, pleasures, and discoveries support an ongoing internal dialogue. A journal can also be a convenient place in which to sketch observations of interesting environments. These sketches are often combined with diagrams and notes that examine the

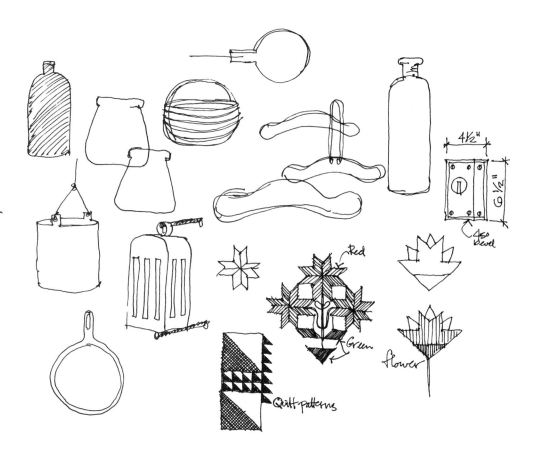

COFFEE

TEA

MILK JUG
(HOT OR COLD)

ideas or lessons within the subject. A journal is also a place to pursue recurring themes over several months or years.

Keeping a journal promotes the visual and verbal expression of thoughts. As journal-writing becomes more of a habit, you might explore a wider range of drawing types and more economical means of visual notation.

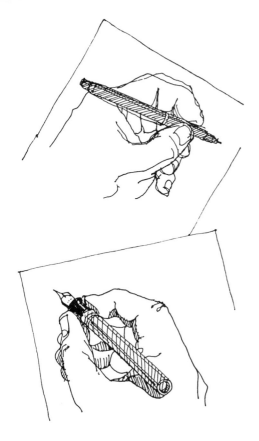

Equipment

The key to learning to sketch is to do it and do it often. This means that you must be ready to sketch anytime, anywhere. Fortunately, the basic equipment for freehand sketching is very simple—a fine-line ink pen or marker and a small pad of paper. Portability is the principal virtue of this equipment, allowing you to take advantage of any opportunity to sketch.

CONSIDERATIONS

All other equipment variations are extensions of the following basic considerations. These suggestions address needs you may develop for variations in scale and visibility of sketches, as well as the durability, utility, and compatibility of your equipment.

Scale: As interest and skills develop, there will usually be a need for larger sheets of paper. You should experiment with different sizes to find those most comfortable and useful to you. In order not to inhibit spontaneity or regularity of sketching, you will have to develop methods or habits to assure that paper is always on hand. Some people keep similar pads in several locations—around the house, at work, or in a briefcase or bag. Others use whatever loose sheets of paper are available and periodically collect them in a folder.

Visibility: To be effective, sketches should be easy to see. Black ink produces clear, high-contrast images. Ink seems to work best on smoothly finished papers. Paper that is too porous will spread ink or snag the point of the pen, resulting in fuzzy, irregular lines. Paper that is too thin may tear or let ink bleed through to the next page.

Durability: Sketching equipment should be capable of producing a permanent record. Fountain pens with jet-black ink are probably the most enduring. Although fine-line markers are very convenient for sketching, the images they produce on paper may deteriorate in varying degrees over time. Until recently, points on most pens or markers would eventually wear down until they were no longer useful. Now there are hard-point markers, such as the Pilot extra fine v-ball, that hold their points and produce a consistent black line. Sketch pads should contain good-quality paper protected by a heavy cover that is not easily bent or torn.

Utility: If a piece of equipment is difficult to use, you will probably avoid using it, thus defeating its purpose. Pens that leak in your pocket, run out of ink, or dry out are a nuisance and discouraging. The cartridge-refill ink pen is one convenient solution to these problems. Another annoyance may be notebooks that are too thick or too large to hold or carry. A spiral binding can be helpful because the rigid cover and used pages can be turned completely back, making the notebook much easier to hold. Avoid general-purpose sketch papers with textured surfaces because your pen will tend to snag.

Compatibility: If you find after a while that any of the suggestions above, or in the rest of this chapter, get in the way of your enjoyment of

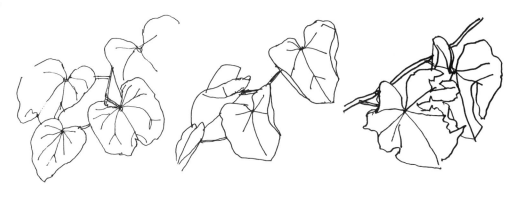

sketching, abandon them at once. If you get a kick out of drawing with a fat marker on paper towels and that leads you to do more sketching, don't hesitate. It is difficult to predict what will motivate different people. Some sketchers may be more comfortable with a certain color of ink or paper. Others may like the feel of a particular pen or paper. Experiment! That is another dimension of the enjoyment of sketching.

PENS

Many brands of fine-line markers produce a clear, dark line and are convenient to carry, but keep in mind that their marks may fade under extensive exposure to light. Broad-tip markers are not very practical for sketches because they are difficult to control and bleed through the paper even more than fine-line markers. The cartridge-ink pen is a good option for people

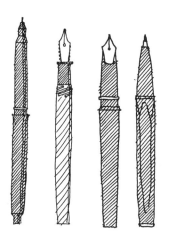 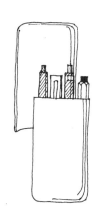 

who prefer a fluid line; it has the added advantage of being less susceptible than markers to blotching or bleeding through the paper. Experience with a variety of pens is the easiest way to find the pen best suited to your particular needs.

You may wish to carry a variety of pens or backup pens and cartridge refills with you, or you may simply want to safeguard against wearing pockets with holes or causing ink stains on your clothes. Some people carry sketching equipment in a camera bag or attaché case.

A less cumbersome option is a container, such as a soft eyeglass or pencil case, or a leather cigar holder, which can easily be carried in a pocket and protects the pens and pencils as well as your clothing.

TRAVEL EQUIPMENT

For working outdoors, sketching trips, or extended travel, you may want to get a little more organized. I have found an airline bag with multiple pockets and a shoulder strap to be particularly well suited. Choose a bag that accepts your largest paper pads in a pocket separate from pens, ink, or anything else that might damage the paper. There should be enough room for other travel equipment—a camera or tape recorder, as well as materials for other media you may try. Getting everything in one bag simplifies handling the equipment and reduces the chances of losing items. To further protect equipment and keep it dry, use resealable plastic bags; they are durable and come in a variety of sizes, including those large enough to hold 9 x 12-inch sketch pads. Depending on time and other circumstances in which you sketch, additional handy equipment may include binder clips to hold back sketch book pages, a couple of sheets of ink blotter, paper towels, a thin, plastic 6-inch ruler, a small glue stick, and a portable stool.

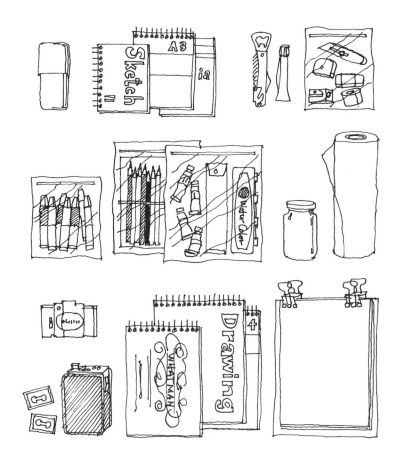

95

Urban scene study for illustration
Michael Doyle

Chapter Five

SKETCHING IN THE STUDIO

The bulk of this book focuses on sketching as a portable, accessible means of observation and notation. But sketches can have an importance and utility long after they were first made. Many designers and artists keep filled sketchbooks in a storage place in their studio or office that is easy to retrieve. Your sketches can be powerful memory triggers of experiences and ideas.

Studios can accommodate additional resources such as computers, scanners, printers, and a range of media that can enhance and extend the utility and impact of sketches. Time is another asset of the studio. You have the space and time to freely explore ideas your sketches evoke. If you hit a snag, you can set the exploration aside and return to it when inspired.

This chapter provides a limited sample of some of the studio-based opportunities for extending the utility of your sketches. You may want to try some of these techniques or explore other possibilities. Above all, pursue your interests and enjoy the process.

Redrawing

Although this sketch showed some interesting qualities, it did not seem to convey the rich variety of textures and patterns in the scene itself. To achieve this, a sheet of tracing paper was laid over the initial sketch. A grid of squares was used to study the composition of the sketch, and the grid was then reproduced in light pencil at double the scale on a separate sheet of paper to guide work on the final drawing.

Experiments in Styles

To stretch your sketching vocabulary, redraw your original sketch to emulate a variety of drawing styles of accomplished designers or illustrators.

Author's sketch

After Paul Hogarth

After Paul Calle

After Alan E. Cober

Digital Editing

Computer applications such as Photoshop can be used to make changes to a scanned image of your sketch. In this example, trees and some details were included in the original sketch to emphasize the principal experiences of framing and depth of the view. These details are eliminated in the modified sketch to focus on the spatial definition.

Original sketch

Modified sketch

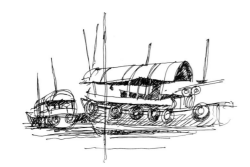

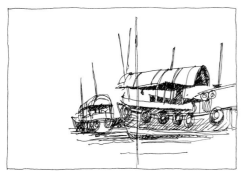

Again using Photoshop, the original sketch (top left) was scanned to create a digital image. Using the *transform* function, the horizontal scale of the image was then altered to create a greater sense of depth. Harbor structures and landscape were then added freehand to provide a context for the boats.

Pencil Rendering

Another form of sketch alteration combines the clarity of line drawings with the subtlety and variety of pencil rendering. Start by photo-copying a line sketch onto paper that has a neutral color, such as a gray or tan with a value midway between light and dark. Add high-lights to the sketch to show color or the effect of sunlight using white- or light-colored pen-cils, and shadows and dark areas with tones of black or dark gray pencils. While there are a variety of colored pencils available for this technique, the rendering on the facing page illustrates the basic effect.

Digital Rendering

There are now several computer graphic applications available that offer a wide choice of rapid rendering techniques that can be applied to line drawings. The original sketch (top right) was scanned at a high resolution (600 dpi) as a bitmap image and converted to gray-tone to allow for rendering. Using Photoshop, a border was placed around the image to form a frame to facilitate different rendering methods. Different values of gray were used to fill the tree, road, and hill areas of the image. A *gradient* tool was used to create a uniform transition from dark to light gray in the sky areas.

CONCLUSION

The intention of this book is to introduce the benefits of adopting the habit and skills of free-hand sketching as providing you access to:

- the study of design and architectural design in particular,
- growth in visual acuity and perception,
- increased facility and fluidity in the design process,
- a means to personal satisfaction.

My hope is that you will be encouraged, as I once was and continue to be, to discover the potential and rewards of freehand drawing. If you open yourself to it, sketching can be an immensely rewarding pursuit, an enriching view not only of the world and people around you, but also an insight into your own perceptions of that world.

Finally, freehand sketching can be a source of simple delight, a process in which you can become completely absorbed. It can be an enjoyable physical experience—the feel of the paper and the movement of the pen across the surface become part of the stimulation and reward of sketching. Accomplished sketchers know that the quality of their drawings ultimately derives from these experiences of awareness, concentration, and touch. If you fully engage in these experiences, you need not worry about the results.

Tarpon Springs

Mykonos (fountain pen and prismacolor on charcoal paper), Kirby Lockard

RECOMMENDED READING

Ching, Francis D. K. *Drawing: A Creative Process.* New York: Van Nostrand Reinhold, 1989 (Wiley).

—— *Sketches from Japan.* New York: Wiley, 2000.

Cooper, Douglas. *Drawing and Perceiving, Third Edition.* New York: Wiley, 2000.

Crowe, Norman and Paul Laseau. *Visual Notes for Architects and Designers.* New York: Wiley, 1997.

Doyle, Michael E. *Color Drawing, Second Edition.* New York: Wiley, 1999.

Edwards, Betty. *The New Drawing on the Right Side of the Brain.* New York: Jeremy P. Tarcher/Putnam, 1999.

—— *Drawing on the Artist Within.* New York: Simon & Schuster, 1987.

Forseth, Kevin. *Rendering the Visual Field.* New York: Van Nostrand Reinhold, 1991 (Wiley).

Hogarth, Paul. *Drawing Architecture: A Creative Approach.* New York: Watson-Guptill, 1973.

—— *Drawing People.* New York, Watson-Guptill, 1971.

Kautzky, Ted. *The Ted Kautzky Pencil Book, comb. ed.* New York: Van Nostrand Reinhold, 1979 (Wiley).

Laseau, Paul. *Graphic Thinking for Architects and Designers, Third Edition.* New York: Wiley, 2000.

—— *Architectural Representation Handbook.* New York: McGraw-Hill, 2000.

Lin, Mike W. *Drawing and Designing with Confidence.* New York: Wiley, 1993.

Lockard, William Kirby. *Design Drawing.* New York: W. W. Norton & Company, 2001.

—— *Design Drawing Experiences.* New York: W. W. Norton & Company, 2001.

Meglin, Nick. *On-the-Spot Drawing.* New York, Watson-Guptill, 1969.

—— with Diane Meglin. *Drawing from Within: Unleashing Your Creative Potential.* New York: Warner, 1999.

Nicolaides, K. *The Natural Way to Draw.* Boston: Houghton-Mifflin, 1975.

Oles, Paul Stevenson. *Architectural Illustration: The Value Delineation Process.* New York: Van Nostrand Reinhold, 1979 (Wiley).

White, Edward T. *Path, Portal, Place: Appreciating Public Space in Urban Environments.* Tallahassee: Architectural Media, 1999.

INDEX